ideals

CHRISTMAS ISSUE

Down the years of memory,
The pageant of Decembers,
Christmas is the miracle
That every heart remembers.

Above the dreaming little towns,
The fields of drifted snow,
There falls the benediction
Of the Christmas star's warm glow.

And heavy hearts grow lighter,
And joyful voices ring,
To celebrate His birthday
And worship Christ, the King.

Alice Mackenzie Swaim

Managing Editor, Ralph Luedtke
Associate Editor, Julie Hogan
Photographic Editor, Gerald Koser
Production Editor, Stuart L. Zyduck

IDEALS—Vol. 34, No. 6—November, MCMLXXVII. Published bimonthly by IDEALS PUBLISHING CORP., 11315 Watertown Plank Road, Milwaukee, Wis. 53226. Second-class postage paid at Milwaukee, Wisconsin. Copyright © MCMLXXVII by IDEALS PUBLISHING CORP. All rights reserved. Title IDEALS registered U.S. Patent Office.

ONE YEAR SUBSCRIPTION—six consecutive issues as published—only $10.00
TWO YEAR SUBSCRIPTION—twelve consecutive issues as published—only $17.00
SINGLE ISSUES—only $2.50

ISBN 0-89542-311-1 250

The First Snow

Robert Freeman Bound

We waited for hours,
As children all will,
After Father had told us
The news with a thrill:

'Twas the oddest sensation
When we'd gaze at the sky;
We seemed to be falling,
But we didn't know why.

Next morning the light
Reflected from snow
Made shimmering patterns
With walls all aglow;

From lowering clouds
And a temperature fall,
The first snow of winter
Would come with a squall.

Then early that evening
The first flakes descended;
And when we retired
The fall hadn't ended.

We looked from our beds
At a white, silent scene
Of tall, pearly trees
And the buildings between.

And our happy, old dog,
With great barking leaps,
Was chasing a rabbit
Through high, snowy heaps.

Oh, the wonderful joy
To be young and know
The thrill of a child
At winter's first snow.

Photo opposite
A. Devaney, Inc.

Snowflakes—A Beautiful Mystery

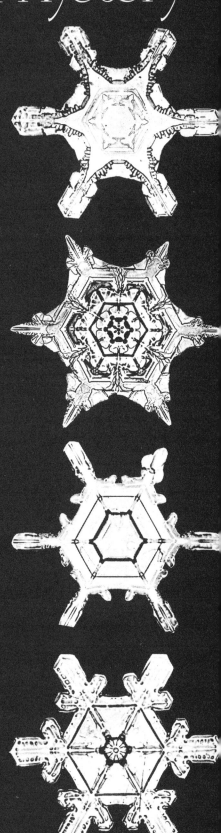

There is a chill wind, the sky lowers and, one by one, snowflakes flutter down. Catching one on his sleeve, a child peers at it, fascinated, until it melts. It is universal—this fascination with snowflakes or "snow blossoms" as they were called by a nineteenth century Japanese snowflake enthusiast. Where do they come from? How are they formed? Are there really no two alike? Questions like these interest not only the artist with his sense of wonder, but also the scientist with his sense of order, and the layperson with his sense of both.

It was such a layperson, Wilson Alwyn Bentley (1865-1931), for whom the study of snowflakes grew from a hobby to an avocation. His interest was first captured when as an adolescent he studied snowflakes under his microscope and tried to draw them. Bentley cultivated this interest through photography until, in his later years, he was accepted by qualified snow researchers as a semiprofessional.

From the infinite number of snowflakes that fell on his Vermont farm, Bentley, of course, studied only a small proportion of them. Yet science respects his assumption, which he expressed as a fact: no two snowflakes are exactly alike. Science (which never assumes anything) is able, nevertheless, to give us some relevant facts with certainty: each flake is an accumulation of crystals, and each crystal could contain about ten sextillion

molecules. What is the chance for these molecules to be arranged alike twice, even in the four billion years since the atmosphere was formed? The odds against it are enormous, mathematicians tell us.

Although Bentley's interest was largely the aspect of design in snowflakes, his enthusiasm helped stimulate research about the beginning and formation of snowflakes. Despite this research, the substance of the core of the snowflake remains a mystery. It may be a minute particle of matter in the atmosphere or a splinter of ice. Whatever it is, it attracts infinitesimal water droplets which are not heavy enough to fall to earth. (A line of 10,000 of these droplets would fit across the head of a pin.) As these droplets crystalize in the proper atmosphere, they set up a field of energy which draws more water vapor. In its own minute storm, the gentle snowflake is born.

As it gains weight, it begins a journey, sometimes as long as six miles, to the earth. Along the way, it is reshaped by the elements through which it passes. When it reaches the earth, it is a unique snowflake which has made a unique journey.

Today Bentley, were he alive, would thrill to the knowledge his avocation promoted. He would see science continuing to progress. But he would see, at the same time, science with art, stand respectfully before the yet unsolved mystery of the beautiful snowflake.

One of the joys of a bygone day
Was driving to town with horse and sleigh.
Down on the river and up the hill
Where the interlacing branches spill

Their patterns over the gleaming snow,
In steady rhythm the horse goes
With hooves clop-clopping, beating time,
To the dancing sleigh bell's tinkling chime.

Sleigh Bells

Rosa Mary Clausen-Mohr

The streets of the old hometown are gay
As friend greets friend from sleigh to sleigh.
Gathered in groups, the hometown folk
Tell the week's news, and laugh, and joke,

Leisurely shopping and getting their mail
Then back again on the homeward trail.
The horses race and the hooves beat fast,
Glad to be going home at last,

While the sleigh bells chatter a happy tune
Of that old-time Saturday afternoon.

SING YE

JOYFUL NOTES

Sing ye joyful, happy notes,
Christmastime is near.
Sing out the olden Yuletide songs
To spread bright, sparkling cheer.

Carol at your neighbors' homes,
For festive, jolly meetings,
And shout "A Merry Christmas, friends!"
That cheeriest of greetings.

Patricia Clafford

Christmas Cookies

Evy Reis

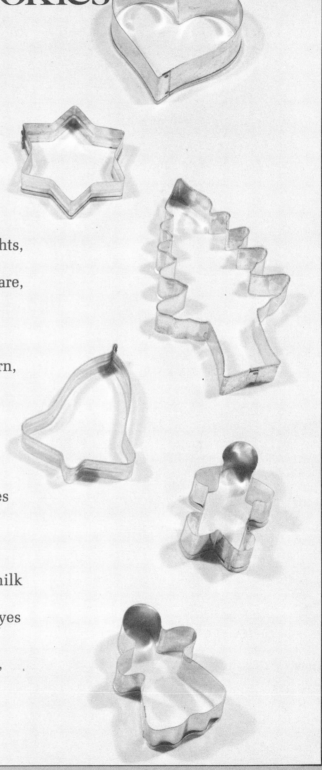

Soon the children will be home
For happy Christmas days.
I'm making "welcome" cookies
In a dozen different ways!

Some are cut just like a star
To remind us of Jesus's birth.
And others like a candle bright
To shine o'er all the earth.

The trees have colored candy lights,
The wreaths a small, red bow.
My dreams are of the love we share,
As I roll and shape the dough.

Some look just like Santa's boot,
This one's a candy cane.
For Tommy there's a sugared horn,
And for Jerry a frosted train!

Julie likes the chocolate bits,
The eyes of gingerbread men;
And Amy always softly says,
"Please pass the plate again."

We'll talk of other Christmastimes
And this new one being born;
Each cookie holds a memory
Of some other Christmas morn.

My cookies and the fresh, cold milk
Are ready to say "hello;"
The laughter and their shining eyes
Give my heart a special glow!

For it's at Mother's kitchen table,
With the oven warmth nearby,
That a family feels its closest
As Christmas Day draws nigh.

Christmas baking is beautifully captured in the design of Marybeth Owens, who created the display for the photo opposite.

At Christmastime

Camilla R. Bittle

At Christmastime when I was small,
　We placed the figure in the stall
(Mary, Blessed Babe, and all),
　Hung mistletoe high in the hall,
Made calendars for kitchen walls,
　And decked our tree with shiny balls.

On Christmas Eve beside the fire,
　We gathered round the wicker chair
To hear our mother's mother read
　Of sugarplums that danced in air,
Of moonlight on new-fallen snow;
　And this we knew—as children know—
Was evidence of love below
　The great high arc of heaven's dome,
Of Christmases secured by home.

The cold—a stabbing, piercing knife,
　The stars—small, dazzling flecks of light,
Our breath rose up in columns white,
　And, oh, the still of Christmas night!

Each year we did the very same,
　Wrote cards, made lists, our cousins came.
On Christmas Eve out caroling,
　Our cheeks bared to the icy sting
Of snowy wind, grew tingling.
　We sang as loud as we could sing.

I ask myself—what did it mean,
  The stockings, tinsel, branches green,
The smell of oranges and pie,
  The wreaths, the bells, the winter sky
Where once a star shone for The Child,
  Whose birth we hailed with praises mild
While overhead the Milky Way
  Was passage for Old Santa's sleigh.

We still hang up the mistletoe.
  My children's faces rosy grow,
Their boots squeak on the hard-packed snow.
  Their eyes with eagerness will glow,
And I'm the only one who'll know
  That it was different long ago.

The tree still flaunts its branches.
  The sky is jet, the stars wink light.
There is a hush to Christmas night;
  The songs are still sung out with might
And Santa's toys, a dazzling sight.

The only thing that's changed is me.
  It's not a fir with lights I see,
For only God can make a tree—
  This is what I see.
And children's eyes can only be
  Small windows on eternity.

And so with gifts, and cousins small,
  And so with garlands in the hall,
And firelight's shadows on the wall—
  God's handiwork, that's all.

Yet in this season of our joy
  There are still those who feel a toy
Is all that matters—not The Boy
  Whose praises we should all employ,
Lest man all brotherhood destroy.

Come, take your stand; decry the whim
  That turkeys, gifts and greetings slim
Define the core—they are the rim
  And but the glossy surface skim,
For in our hearts we kneel to Him.

The Story of the Holly Sprig

By Arthur Upson

"I 'D be the shiniest green,"
　　Wished once a sprig of holly,
"That e'er at Yule was seen,
　　And deck some banquet jolly!"

"I 'd be the cheeriest red,"
　　Wished once the holly-berry,
"That e'er at board rich spread
　　Helped make the feasters merry!"

The life within them heard
　　Down dark and silent courses,
For each wish is a word
　　To those fair-hidden sources.

All Summer in the wood,
　　While they were riper growing,
The deep roots understood,
　　And helped without their knowing.

In a little market stall
　　At Yule the sprig lay waiting,
For fine folk one and all
　　Passed by that open grating.

The Eve of Christmas Day
　　It had been passed by many,
When one turned not away
　　And bought it for a penny.

Hers was a home of care
　　Which not a wreath made jolly;
The only Christmas there
　　Was that sweet sprig of holly.

"Oh, this is better far
　　Than banquet!" thought the berry;
The leaves glowed like a star
　　And made that cottage merry!

Photo opposite
Gene Ahrens

From *St. Nicholas* Magazine, c. 1907.

Festive December

WINTER COMES TO STILLMEADOW, sifting down with the sifting snow. The snowfall gives a strange impermanence to the countryside, blurring the far hills, silvering the pond, tipping the mailbox with ermine. The air itself seems silver-white. When I go out to fill the bird feeders, starry flakes melt cool on my cheeks.

The chickadees chatter, nuthatches slide down the tree trunks, blue jays cry angrily from the sugar maples. Juncos are almost under my feet. The relationship of birds and man is a rewarding one, for even the shiest birds respond to friendship. The bridge between me and mine is an easy one, composed of sunflower seeds, chick feed, raisins, bread crumbs, suet cakes. As I talk to the gathering wings, I am answered by the dipping toward my hands. I cannot help thinking that barriers between people—of all nationalities—should not be insurmountable, for human beings are of one species. Perhaps the secret is in personal giving. What is held out in the open hand means more than allotments.

The valley begins to look festive as December goes along. The giant pine at the village center glows with light. Christmas wreaths blossom on every door. George Tomey decorates the market, and Green's store looks like a Christmas party. The post office is piled so high with packages that I can barely see the heads of the postal workers.

As Christmas approaches, Erma helps me decorate Stillmeadow. Mistletoe, holly and pine branches give a festive look to the old house. Gay greeting cards decorate two of the mantels, the corner cupboard where I keep the milk glass, and the bookshelves. Christmas candles go on the wide window ledges but never on the tree, for I am afraid they might start a fire. Bowls of fruit are temporary decorations, for the children start to eat the fruit as soon as they arrive for the holidays, and the bowl on the coffee bench has to be refilled several times a day.

The tree goes in the front living room, and we put our packages under it. Christmas Eve is my special time. When the children were growing up, Jill used to pop corn and set out the wooden dough trough, filled with nuts and polished apples, while I read Dickens's *A Christmas Carol* aloud. I know it by heart because it was

read to me every Christmas when I was growing up. It was a link between the generations. Nowadays, however, the very young do not make for quiet reading. Even after they are tucked away, they want a drink of water, or they lose their go-to-sleep rabbit over the crib wall, or *something*.

But after they finally go to sleep, the adults sit around the fire and sing carols and talk. I have a chance to look at the three grown-up children—my daughter, and Jill's son and daughter—and they are beautiful to me. Their young thoughtful faces have not really changed.

How far they have traveled since *they* were asking for a drink of water at bedtime! And how proud I am of them. Sometimes when I go out to the back kitchen to let Holly in, I imagine the drying bunny suits and mittens and hoods belong to my three. Time is a curious thing. Those bunny suits belong to Muffin, Anne, Jamie, and Betsy, and the larger snow outfits to the two older grandchildren (who also have ice skates, for fun on the pond).

This is an uneasy world, but at this holy time I find faith anew in the power of love and good-will. My belief in goodness is not shaken. The Babe born in a manger brought an enduring message to mankind. He was indeed to become the Prince of Peace, and is so still.

The snow stops falling, and the lovely light of a distant untroubled moon makes magic in swamp and meadow. The house settles into quiet. I go out with the cockers and Irish for a last look at night. On Christmas Eve my Honey—the golden cocker who companioned me for fourteen years—moves beside me. Jill stands in the lighted doorway. Remembrance is a form of meeting, says Gibran, and so it is.

Inevitably, as I turn out the lights and the embers die into ash, Connie comes softly down the stairs. "I just wanted to say what a lovely Christmas Eve, Mamma," she says. And this, of course, is my best present of all.

I think of neighbors I have never seen, all over the world, and pray for peace and goodwill for us all.

Gladys Taber

The Christmas Story

 n those days Mary arose and went with haste into the hill country, to a city of Judah,

and she entered the house of Zechariah and greeted Elizabeth.

And when Elizabeth heard the greeting of Mary, the babe leaped in her womb; and Elizabeth was filled with the Holy Spirit

and she exclaimed with a loud cry, "Blessed are you among women, and blessed is the fruit of your womb!"

Luke 1:39-42

 n those days a decree went out from Caesar Augustus that all the world should be enrolled.

This was the first enrollment, when Quirinius was the governor of Syria.

And all went to be enrolled, each to his own city.

And Joseph also went up from Galilee, from the city of Nazareth, to Judea, to the city of David, which is called Bethlehem, because he was of the house and lineage of David, to be enrolled with Mary, his betrothed, who was with child.

And while they were there, the time came for her to be delivered.

And she gave birth to her first-born son and wrapped him in swaddling cloths, and laid him in a manger, because there was no place for them in the inn.

Luke 2:1-7

Painting opposite
ADORATION OF THE CHILD
Gerard von Honthorst
1590-1656
(Photo: Three Lions, Inc.)

nd in that region there were shepherds out in the field, keeping watch over their flock by night.

And an angel of the Lord appeared to them, and the glory of the Lord shone around them, and they were filled with fear.

And the angel said to them, "Be not afraid; for behold, I bring you good news of a great joy which will come to all the people;

for to you is born this day in the city of David a Savior, who is Christ the Lord.

And this will be a sign for you: you will find a babe wrapped in swaddling cloths and lying in a manger."

And suddenly there was with the angel a multitude of the heavenly host praising God and saying,

"Glory to God in the highest, and on earth peace among men with whom he is pleased!"

Luke 2:8-14

 hen the angels went away from them into heaven, the shepherds said to one another, "Let us go over to Bethlehem and see this thing that has happened, which the Lord has made known to us."

And they went with haste, and found Mary and Joseph, and the babe lying in a manger.

Luke 2:15-16

ow when Jesus was born in Bethlehem of Judea in the days of Herod the king, behold, wise men from the East came to Jerusalem, saying,

"Where is he who has been born king of the Jews? For we have seen his star in the East, and have come to worship him."

When they had heard the king they went their way; and lo, the star which they had seen in the East went before them, till it came to rest over the place where the child was.

When they saw the star, they rejoiced exceedingly with great joy;

and going into the house they saw the child with Mary his mother, and they fell down and worshiped him. Then, opening their treasures, they offered him gifts, gold and frankincense and myrrh.

Matt. 2:1-2, 9-11

ow when they had departed, behold, an angel of the Lord appeared to Joseph in a dream and said, "Rise, take the child and his mother, and flee to Egypt, and remain there till I tell you; for Herod is about to search for the child, to destroy him."

And he rose and took the child and his mother by night, and departed to Egypt,

and remained there until the death of Herod. This was to fulfill what the Lord had spoken by the prophet, "Out of Egypt have I called my son."

Matt. 2:13-15

Christmas Cards

This time of year, I always stand
Beside the door to wait
Until I hear the postman lift
The latch upon the gate.
I run to meet him, for I know
He will most certainly
Reach down into his sack to find
Some Christmas cards for me.

In many shapes and sizes,
They come from far and near,
And each of them recalls a face
And friendship very dear.
Some come in bright red envelopes
With hollyberry seals,
And others may arrive in white
With scenes of winter fields.

And then there are the special ones,
With edges trimmed in gold,
Much too thick, and long, and wide
For my mailbox to hold.
I watch the stack grow larger,
With humble joy, to see
The many folks throughout the year
Who have remembered me.

And sitting at my rosewood desk
Till long into the night,
I choose my own cards carefully;
And then I start to write.
My heart is filled with memories,
Bright as a candle flame,
And I address the envelopes,
But love's hand signs my name.

Grace E. Easley

Dear Santa

I guess you know
It's the time of the year
When everyone's happy
And sending good cheer.

When you come to our house,
There you will see
Two bright red stockings,
Lights and a tree.

In the kitchen,
Cake and candy, too,
With a note that says,
"Just for you!"

I've been a good girl,
Waiting for you.
PS Bring something for
My sister, too!

Marcella Denise Simon

A Rest for Santa

You must be tired, Santa,
You've worked the whole night through;
So sit and rest a moment
And eat a little, too.

I made the cookies specially
And surely hope you'll find
That each and every one of them
Is quite your favorite kind.

And when you lift your pack again
And hurry on your way,
Take with you all our wishes
For a happy Christmas Day.

Virginia Blanck Moore

My Christmas Stocking

LaVerne P. Larson

Each Christmas Eve when I was small
I'd hang my stocking there,
Right above the chimney place,
With special, loving care.

My heart was filled with hopes and dreams
Of things it would contain:
Goodies of every sort
Straight from Santa's lane.

I'd climb into my bed; and then,
With covers round my chin,
I would fall fast asleep
And always dream of him.

And sure enough, on Christmas morn
When I dashed from my bed,
Dear old Santa had been there
Just as my folks had said.

I'd shout with glee and jump for joy
As the goodies tumbled out;
Yes, my lovely Christmas stocking
Was a gem to dream about.

I loved the tree with ornaments
And the pretty twinkling lights;
But my lumpy Christmas stocking
Gave me the most and best delight.

Photo opposite
Alpha Photo Associates

A Bedtime Memory

I remember well,
When I was small,
The times upon Dad's knee;
He held me long,
And I would sit
And he would read to me.

Those days, now gone,
I do recall
With happy memory;
As I hold my child
While he sits
So still upon my knee.

Molly Allison

Christmas Eves
Remembered

Gay, twinkling, ornaments tonight,
Like jewels, hang on the tree.
They seem to lead me by the hand
Down the lane of memory.

I am a little child again . . .
Our tree with candlelight
Sends out a cheer to all who pass
Our house on Christmas night.

Mother plays the organ, we sing
The carols of famed renown,
And listen to the church bells ring
Across the snow-wrapped town.

Dad tells us of the wise men
Who follow a bright star;
How it guides them to a manger
Where Mary and Jesus are.

Gay, twinkling ornaments tonight,
Like jewels, hang on the tree.
They seem to lead me by the hand
Down the lane of memory!

Bettie Payne Welles

Secrets

Santa is coming and secrets abound
When he gets to your house
He won't make a sound;
But, oh, the lovely things on his back,
Bulging and tumbling out of his pack,
As he comes down the chimney,
Or through your front door,
And places them there
By your tree on the floor.
What a jolly old man—but he cannot tarry
Though he wishes you joy
And a Christmas that's merry.

Loris Griffin

Santa's Workshop

All the elves in Santa's workshop
    Are a very busy lot;
As for toys for all the children
    They are Johnny-on-the-spot.

Santa reads his many letters
    And then tells his trusty elves
Just what toys to manufacture;
    Then they stock the spacious shelves.

There are dolls that walk and chatter,
    There are skateboards by the scores,
There are wagons, trains and ice skates
    And so many, many more.

And the thing that fascinates me
    Is the fact that every year
There are more than just enough toys
    For all the children dear.

Georgia B. Adams

*The whimsical little people shown in the photo opposite were made by
Betty Brown of Mequon, Wisconsin.*

Is There a Santa Claus?

By popular demand, we are again featuring this famous editorial which first appeared in THE SUN, September 21, 1897.

We take pleasure in answering at once and thus prominently the communication below, expressing at the same time our great gratification that its faithful author is numbered among the friends of *The Sun:*

Dear Editor:

I am 8 years old.
Some of my little friends say there is no Santa Claus.
Papa says, ''If you see it in *The Sun* it's so.''
Please tell me the truth, is there a Santa Claus?

> Virginia O'Hanlon,
> 115 West 95th Street

Virginia, your little friends are wrong. They have been affected by the skepticism of a skeptical age. They do not believe except they see. They think that nothing can be which is not comprehensible by their little minds. All minds, Virginia, whether they be men's or children's, are little. In this great universe of ours man is a mere insect, an ant, in his intellect, as compared with the boundless world about him, as measured by the intelligence capable of grasping the whole of truth and knowledge.

Yes, Virginia, there is a Santa Claus. He exists as certainly as love and generosity and devotion exist; and you know that they abound and give to your life its highest beauty and joy. Alas! how dreary would be the world if there were no Santa Claus! It would be as dreary as if there were no Virginias. There would be no

childlike faith then, no poetry, no romance to make tolerable this existence. We should have no enjoyment, except in sense and sight. The eternal light with which childhood fills the world would be extinguished.

Not believe in Santa Claus! You might as well not believe in fairies! You might get your papa to hire men to watch in all the chimneys on Christmas Eve to catch Santa Claus, but even if they did not see Santa Claus coming down, what would that prove? Nobody sees Santa Claus, but that is no sign that there is no Santa Claus. The most real things in the world are those that neither children nor men can see. Did you ever see fairies dancing on the lawn? Of course not, but that's no proof that they are not there. Nobody can conceive or imagine all the wonders there are unseen and unseeable in the world.

You tear apart the baby's rattle and see what makes the noise inside; but there is a veil covering the unseen world which not the strongest man, nor even the united strength of all the strongest men that ever lived, could tear apart. Only faith, fancy, poetry, love, romance, can push aside that curtain and view and picture the supernal beauty and glory beyond. Is it all real? Ah, Virginia, in all this world there is nothing else real and abiding.

No Santa Claus! Thank God he lives, and he lives forever. A thousand years from now, Virginia, nay, ten times ten thousand years from now, he will continue to make glad the heart of childhood.

Francis P. Church

How Did
Santa Know?

Georgia B. Adams

He was a plump, round Santa Claus,
   His whiskers white as snow;
And as we stood to wait our turn,
   Our wishes to make known,
We tried to think of all the times
   We minded Mom and Dad
And never disobeyed just once
   Despite the fun we had.

We had a hundred reasons why
   Santa should come our way,
But when we climbed upon his knee
   We forgot what to say!
He stroked his long and flowing beard,
   And with a twinkling eye,
He promised to remember us
   As he was passing by.

We couldn't remember that bright train
   And doll we wanted so;
And yet on Christmas morning there
   Were all the gifts. And, lo,
There were so many more things, too—
   He knew what to bestow.
We figure he's a wise, old man;
   But how did Santa know?

How Do the Animals

Spend the Winter?

Julia F. Lieser

How will you spend the winter? If you are like most boys and girls, you will spend much of your time going to school. During your time off you will play. When there is snow you will go sledding, make snowmen, and have snowball fights. When it is very cold, you will ice-skate and play ice hockey. And when it is very, very cold you will stay snug and warm in your comfortable home.

But what if you could ask a little cottontail rabbit how he was going to spend the winter? His answer would be quite different from yours.

First of all, he has no warm, comfy house to go to when cold wind and snow come. He doesn't even have a warm nest or a supply of food to tide him over. He must find a brush pile or some tangled plants. Sitting beneath them will give him some protection from wind and snow. He can nibble on twigs and stems from the inside when he becomes very hungry.

When the weather turns warm, he will leave his hiding place to look for something more tasty in the way of food. If he is unlucky, he will become a meal for a fox, lynx, bobcat, or hawk. But if he is lucky, he will return to this brush pile to wait for spring.

The opossum isn't any more fortunate than the cottontail when it comes to winter shelter. The opossum prepares himself no cozy nest to wait out winter. He must find a new place to settle down when he is cold and sleepy. He may sleep out a cold spell in a hollow tree or a hollow log.

The day always comes when hunger pangs can no longer be ignored and he must go forth, risking frostbite on his naked ears and long, bare tail. The opossum will eat almost anything, but food of any kind is scarce in winter and the opossum rarely has a full stomach until spring.

The tree squirrels are warmly content, even in

the most severe weather, sleeping in their leaf-lined, hollow-tree nests. On most any day you can find squirrel tracks in the snow, made by hungry squirrels. But they have only to remember where they buried nuts and acorns the previous fall, and they will not go hungry.

The chipmunk does not like cold weather. In his underground home, down below the frost line, he sleeps away the winter. In his tiny bedroom he relaxes on a bed of leaves placed on top of his food supply. Every now and then the sleepy chipmunk half awakens, reaches for a snack, then dozes off again.

The chipmunk is a light sleeper, but the groundhog or woodchuck is a heavy winter sleeper. He, too, sleeps on a soft bed of leaves down below the frost line. But he does not store food in his bedroom. Instead, he eats heavily in the fall and adds a heavy layer of fat under his skin. He sleeps the deep sleep of hibernation, not waking until spring. His extra fat sustains him while he sleeps.

The beaver spends his winter days sitting in his warm, cozy lodge in the middle of the pond or stream. He spent much time in the fall adding sticks and plastering them with mud, making his home tight and secure and able to keep out wind and snow. He has a private underwater entrance, so he has little trouble with intruders. At the bottom of the pond under the lodge is his private food supply, logs and sticks, anchored into the mud. He spends a lot of time relaxing and dozing.

The raccoon has a warm nest, usually high in a hollow tree. Sometimes several raccoons will share a nest and help to keep each other warm. They may sleep for several days at a time if the weather is severe. When they go food hunting they don't find much—a field mouse or a careless bird, or maybe a fish in an unfrozen stream. So the raccoons head for home and sleep some more.

The field mice are active day and night, summer and winter. They hunt for food, but if they don't find any, they hurry home to an overstocked, underground larder. The meadow jumping mice are sleeping in their deep burrows, long tails coiled beneath them and a layer of fat to sustain them. They are the only members of the mice family to hibernate.

''And how will you spend the winter?'' If you could ask your wild animal friends, their answers would be quite different from yours.

It's a Great Night

It's a great night for gathering round the fire
    And spinning a yarn or two;
It's grand to be cozily snuggled up in
    A favorite armchair, too.

It's snowing without, and the winds do howl;
    How comfortable by the fire!
See how the shadows are cast on the walls
    As the flames lick up still higher.

In due time we'll roast chestnuts by the fire,
    What a choice morsel they'll make!
We might run through photograph albums then
    Just for the old-time's sake!

We'll talk of our friends and our blessings, too,
    And the beauties of true goodwill;
It's a great night for gathering round the fire
    While the winds outside grow chill.

Georgia B. Adams

Photo opposite
Freelance Photographers Guild

Home for Christmas

The folks will be there waiting
With a smile and open arms;
I'll find warmth and laughter there,
The wealth of homey charms.

Away from the busy sights and sounds
I take the road toward home,
Back to the hills and the valleys,
Back where I loved to roam.

There'll be a Christmas tree in the window
As friends and neighbors gather round
To sing the songs of Christmas;
And joy shall there abound.

The snow is white and glistening,
The stars shine bright above;
I'm going home for Christmas,
Home to those I love.

The road seems long and winding
But there's happiness at the end;
For I'm going home for Christmas,
And home is round the bend.

Gladys Billings Bratton

Mistletoe for Grandpa

Sprigs of Christmas mistletoe
Would tickle Grandpa's fancy so
That Grandma placed it everywhere,
In satin ribbons tied with care.

And each year loved ones passing by
Would share a kiss and wink an eye
In warmest family fellowship
Then, smiling, watch dear Grandpa slip
One tiny sprig of mistletoe
In Grandma's curling crown of snow
And see him kiss her tenderly
Beneath the brightly shining tree.

Vivian Marie Chapman

T H E R O A D , - W I N T E R .

A LOOK BACK AT

POCAHONTAS.   LANCET.   PRINCE.   GREY EDDY.   GENERAL DARCY.   FLORA TEMPLE.   LANTERN.   LADY WOODRUFF.   BROWN DICK.   ALICE GREY.   STELLA.

"TROTTING CRACKS" ON THE SNOW.

AMERICA'S SLED AND SLEIGH DAYS

Mary Carolyn McKee

Of the hundreds of Currier & Ives prints portraying American life a century or so ago, the most popular of all were, and are, the winter scenes. These snowscapes, although somewhat sentimentalized, presented an authentic record of winter living, and many of them featured the vehicles that were then the common means of transport for nearly everyone: sleds and sleighs. Back when the ''gasoline buggy'' was far in the future and the snowmobile not even a dream, many people looked forward to hitching up these carriers for local travel over the snow.

Winter travel on runners was much faster and easier in many parts of the country than travel on wheels in the summer when roads were deeply rutted and, when rains were heavy, turned into rivers of mud. On farms, large sleds were used to haul blocks of ice from ponds, logs from the woods, and feed for the stock. With their floors covered with straw or blankets, the sleds carried families to market, to church services, and on neighborhood visits. Lighter and often quite elegant sleighs were used for party-going or simply for the fun of racing along snow-covered roads.

According to early accounts, the forerunner of these

versatile winter vehicles was a crude ground sled or ''drag'' invented by the American Indians. It consisted of two poles connected with another pole or a platform of sticks. Sometimes a hide basket was lashed to these crosspieces. On these simple sleds the Indians hauled firewood, animals killed in the hunt, and even tents. Since they were usually quite narrow, they could be pulled along the forest trails by hand using thongs, or the thongs could be hitched to a dog or horse.

Early American farm sleds were almost as primitive. Two pieces of wood were shaped into runners and fastened together with slats. Later, wooden or metal runners were attached to box-like wagon beds.

The first sleighs, like most of the carriages and coaches in colonial days, were heavy and cumbersome until an enterprising young man from Connecticut revolutionized sleigh styles in the early nineteenth century. James Brewster, a descendant of Elder Brewster of *Mayflower* fame, was apprenticed to a Massachusetts carriage builder for a number of years. In 1809 he had set out for New York City by stagecoach to seek another position. When the coach broke down in New Haven, Connecticut, and the passengers had to wait for repairs, Brewster walked about town and chanced to meet the owner of the town's first carriage company. When the builder offered him a job, he accepted it and forgot about New York.

Within a year he had launched his own carriage and sleigh business in New Haven. Brewster sleighs were marvels of grace and style as they skimmed lightly over the snow. There were models with one and two seats. More elaborate sleighs provided a seat for the coachman, and there were small ''pony sleighs'' to delight children. There were even ''push sleighs'' to be occupied by warmly dressed ladies and propelled from behind over the ice of ponds and lakes by their escorts on skates.

Sleighs and sleigh bells were natural companions, for sleigh bells were to sleighs as horns are to automobiles. On winter evenings they prevented collisions, warned pedestrians, and filled the winter air with their cheerful sounds. Sleigh bells became big business in East Hampton, Connecticut, where William Barton started making them about 1808. At one time there were at least thirty bell companies in town and East Hampton became popularly known as ''Jingletown.'' The bells came in a variety of sizes and patterns and were either single- or double-throated. The single-throated type had one slit to let out the sound; the double-throated variety had two slits cutting across each other at right angles. There were some twenty sizes of common sleigh bells, ranging from seven-eighths of an inch in diameter to more than three inches. They were strung together and sold by the pound, or riveted to the neck- or body-straps of a horse. Bells with the sweetest tone were cast from ''bell metal,'' a combination of tin and copper. Other less expensive versions were simply stamped out of steel or brass.

There was always something wonderfully exhilarating about the ring of sleigh bells across a winter landscape. Edgar Allan Poe expressed this in the first stanza of *The Bells:*

> *Here the sledges with the bells—*
> *Silver bells!*
> *What a world of merriment their*
> *melody foretells!*
> *How they tinkle, tinkle, tinkle*
> *In the icy air of night*
> *While the stars that oversprinkle*
> *All the heavens, seem to twinkle*
> *With a crystalline delight . . . .*

Some years after Poe's poem appeared, J. S. Pierpont, a minister from Litchfield, Connecticut, paid tribute to the joys of sleighing. He wrote for a Sunday School entertainment one of the most popular winter songs ever written. His *Jingle Bells* catches the high spirits of sleigh riders who glide over the snow on a winter evening:

> *Dashing through the snow*
> *In a one-horse open sleigh,*
> *O'er the fields we go*
> *Laughing all the way;*
> *Bells on bobtail ring,*
> *Making spirits bright;*
> *What fun it is to ride and sing*
> *A sleighing song tonight.*

That the jingle of the bells was reassuring after a storm is pointed out in John Greenleaf Whittier's *Snowbound.* In the morning following the great snowfall, all was silent until the shut-ins ''heard once more the sleigh bells' sound,'' and knew that soon life would be back to normal.

Sleighing was all the rage in America from about 1830 to almost the end of the century, and it gave the streets of cities such as New York and Boston the look of a gala winter festival. Stable owners welcomed weather that would bring a rush of business—horses were groomed, sleighs made ready, and harness polished when the air ''smelled like snow.''

Daring young drivers often raced their sleighs in areas of suburban Boston. Occasionally there were smash-ups due to the heady combinations of fast

Entered according to act of Congress in the Year 1859 by Currier & Ives, in the Clerk's Office of the Distt Court of the Southern Distt of N.Y.   REPRINTED FROM LITH. BY CURRIER & IVES.

THE SLEIGH RACE.

horses and speedy sleighs, but the popular sport thrived. Two huge sleighs, "Cleopatra's Barge" and the "Mammoth Mayflower," cruised the streets of the Massachusetts capital after a big snowfall. Both resembled ships mounted upon runners and were drawn by several teams of strong horses. They often carried cargoes of more than twenty passengers around the city or out into the country.

It should be noted that not quite everyone considered sleighing a delightful pastime. Harriet Martineau, a British writer who visited America in the late 1830s and wrote *Retrospect of Western Travel* was a dissenter. She described the sport: "Set your chair on a springboard out on the porch; put your feet in a pail full of powdered ice; have somebody jingle a bell in one ear and somebody blow into the other with a bellows, and you will have an exact idea of sleighing."

However, Charles Dickens, who visited America in 1867 (his second journey), had an entirely different reaction. He chanced to be in New York City during a snowstorm that was severe enough to stop train service for a time. In a letter to one of his daughters, Dickens described the city streets as bordered with high walls of sparkling ice and, ever delighted with a dramatic situation, wrote, "I turned out in a rather gorgeous sleigh yesterday with any quantity of buffalo robes and made an imposing appearance."

The use of sleds and sleighs continued through the 1890s but slowly waned after the turn of the century. As late as 1902 the Sears & Roebuck catalog featured a "cutter" department with illustrations of two one-horse vehicles priced at $16.90 and $22.50. A two-seated "Russian" bob sleigh was offered for $46.90.

Today one occasionally sees horse-drawn sleighs gliding along the side roads in New England, the Pennsylvania Dutch country, and the Middle West. The delight of antiques collectors, they add a nostalgic Currier & Ives touch to the snowscape.

One of this writer's earliest winter recollections was watching a cutter dash down a Missouri lane. With bells a-jingle, it drew up with a burst of speed before our gate. My uncle and aunt and their two small boys threw aside the fur robe and stepped out.

What a thrilling arrival that was! And what an exciting memory!

From the December 1974 issue of EARLY AMERICAN LIFE. Used with permission.

"a Christmas Kitten"

Our Christmas kitten's really bright;
   She's standing guard this Christmas night.
Sometimes she jumps from stair to stair,
   Or hides beneath the rocking chair.

She's keeping watch from dusk till dawn;
   Something moves and the chase is on!
Papers rustle in a box:
   A search is made of Christmas socks.

      A toy mouse, a catnip ball,
         Some scraps of yarn out in the hall,
      The Christmas crèche, a cookie plate,
         All these she must investigate.

      But not just now; it's time for bed;
         A place to lay her weary head.
      Content this is the place for her,
         She drops her guard and starts to purr!

Alice Leedy Mason

Photo opposite
Clifford Carroll

Winter Fun

Edna Jaques

Over the hills we go coasting down,
Then across the lake like a mirror round;
On the smooth white slope we start, from above,
Then down we go as swift as a dove.

Out in the yard right by our gate
The big, white snowman we like to make.
We shape it with snow, white and clean;
With fir moss for a beard
It's just the thing.
A carrot for a nose and apples for eyes,
It makes him look so very wise.

Down on the pond there is everyone
Skating together; oh, what fun!
A figure eight, a tug of war,
There's a bonfire blazing on the shore.

We'll warm our hands before we run;
There's hot chocolate waiting for everyone.
We'll sing together for good cheer;
It's the merriest, happiest time of the year.

Skating Pond

Irene Lloyd Goodwin

They dart about like water bugs
   With waving arms and sprawling legs,
Some as graceful as the swans
   While others stiff as wooden pegs,
And yet the fun they have is worth
   More than the minted gold of earth.

The ice is clear as painted glass,
   Bordered by heaps of drifted snow,
The winter sky above the trees
   Almost as blue as indigo,
A setting lovely as a gem
   Set in a vacant lot for them.

They swoop, and dip, and whirl, and dart,
   Fall with a thud and slide a bit,
Crawl on all fours like tiny bears,
   Yet never seem to tire of it
But up and at it once again,
   Crusted with snow like frozen men.

Their little cheeks are warm and red,
   Like apples on the rosy side,
Snowsuits of red, and green, and blue—
   The little bodies tucked inside
Are warm as kittens wrapped in wool:
   Lovely to look at . . . beautiful.

Here on this vacant lot is heard
   Young laughter merry as a lark,
The gay voice of a little girl,
   A tiny dog's excited bark,
Where all the bells of heaven chime
   Under the spell of wintertime.

"a Christmas Pup"

Oh, what an absolute delight!
   Just see what happened Christmas night.
A tiny pup—cute, wiggly, smart—
   Came right into my eager heart.

I said ''hello'' and picked him up;
   He was such a naughty pup.
He yawned and tried to get away
   Because he thought he'd rather play.

So much to see, so many lights,
   A dozen other tempting sights;
He had to wrestle with the rug
   Before he paused to give a hug.

He gave each ornament a sniff,
   Then tore the bows from every gift.
Worn out at last, he came my way
   And love came in my heart to stay.

Alice Leedy Mason

Photo opposite
Clifford Carroll

from the editor's scrapbook

From every spire on Christmas Eve the Christmas bells ring out their message of goodwill and cheer.

Eleanor Hunter

Blessed is the season which engages the whole world in a conspiracy of love.

Hamilton Wright Mabie

How can you make this the happiest Christmas of your life? Simply by trying to give yourself to others. Put something of yourself into everything you give. A gift, however small, speaks its own language. And when it tells of the love of the giver, it is truly blessed.

Norman Vincent Peale

Christmas is the time to let your heart do the thinking.

Patricia Clafford

Joy is a flame which association alone can keep alive and which goes out unless communicated.

Lamartine

The earth has grown old with its burden of care,
But at Christmas it always is young;
The heart of the jewel burns lustrous and fair
And its soul full of music breaks forth on the air,
When the song of the angels is sung.

Phillips Brooks

At Christmastide the open hand
Scatters its bounty o'er sea and land;
And none are left to grieve alone,
For love is heaven and claims its own.

Margaret E. Sangster

The joy of brightening other lives, bearing others' burdens, easing others' loads and supplanting empty hearts and lives with generous gifts becomes for us the magic of Christmas.

W. C. Jones

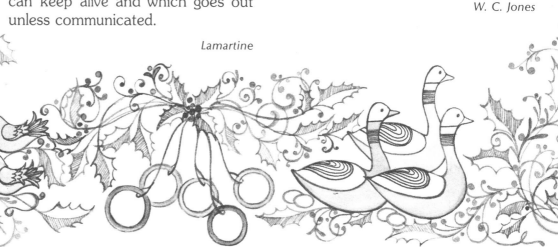

Love came down at Christmas,
Love all lovely, love divine;
Love was born at Christmas.

Christina Rossetti

Kindness is like snow . . . it will make
beautiful anything it covers.

Author Unknown

God rest ye, merry gentlemen!
Let nothing you dismay,
For Jesus Christ, our Saviour,
Was born on Christmas Day.

Dinah Maria Mulock Craik

Familes find themselves at Christmas.
The true spirit of Christmas is much
more perfectly expressed around the
fireside than in the bustle of holiday
commerce.

Author Unknown

If Winter comes, can Spring be far
behind?

P. B. Shelley

God so loved the world, that he gave
his only begotten Son, that whoso-
ever believeth in him should not
perish, but have everlasting life.

John 3:16

And it was always said of him, that he
knew how to keep Christmas well . . .
May that be truly said of us, and all of
us! And so, as Tiny Tim observed,
God bless us, Every One!

Charles Dickens

Christmas is the shining festival of the
unselfish . . . it is the homecoming of
the spirit . . . the glorification of all that
is good.

Author Unknown

Always repay kindness with even
more kindness.

Welsh Proverb

The gift without the giver is bare; who
gives of himself with his alms feeds
three: himself, his hungering neighbor,
and me.

James Russell Lowell

On Christmas Day

I've gotten many gifts this day
From kin and loved ones true,
But there are other gifts I have
Which should be counted, too.

In other words, I have from you
A love that e'er abides;
I have the faith you have in me,
That speaks low and confides.

I have a deep respect that comes
From years of friendship, friend;
I have a trust you've placed in me,
On me you do depend.

I have the joy that bubbles o'er
From your heart into mine;
Now gifts material do please,
And these are very fine,

But I just go one step ahead.
Beyond these gifts I see
The worth of one good, honest friend;
The good friend you're to me!

Georgia B. Adams

TUCKER CHINA
A native American porcelain: still highly prized but frequently misidentified

A century and a half ago a young Quaker named William Ellis Tucker set out to become the first American to produce a porcelain that could successfully compete with imports from Europe and Asia. His father, Benjamin Tucker, proprietor of a Philadelphia shop selling imported china, provided a kiln, materials—native kaolin, feldspar, a fine blue clay—and space for his son's experiments in the yard behind the shop. William ground, mixed, formed, glazed, and fired his ingredients. After numerous failures he finally hit upon a "secret formula" for making a porcelain that was hard, translucent, and heat-resistant. In 1826 father and son began manufacturing what became known as Tucker china.

The Tucker china works successfully made and sold porcelain for a scant twelve years, but during its short life the factory brought American porcelain making to a high degree of perfection. In 1827 William Tucker took a prize at the Franklin Institute in Philadelphia for "the best specimen of *porcelain* to be made in Pennsylvania." In 1828 he won a silver medal for "the best porcelain made in the United States." In those days a simple Tucker pitcher cost thirty-seven and a half cents; an ambitious vase, a dollar fifty. Now an example of Tucker can fetch hundreds of dollars at auction—a sign that collectors still prize the ware. Tucker is handsome, and it played an important role in our past. It is also often challenging to identify, but the search for authentication can be as rewarding as the pride of ownership.

Identifying Tucker china is easiest when a mark is present. Tucker marks consisted of either the firm's name or the initial of a workman. The firm's name, often hand printed in red under the glaze, changed over the years from William Ellis Tucker to Tucker & Hulme to Joseph Hemphill, with variations. The workman's marks that are positively known are B or C.B. for Charles J. Boulter; F for Charles Frederick; H for William Hand (an Englishman); M for Joseph Morgan; V for an artist known as Vivian (a Frenchman); and W for Andrew Craig Walker, thought to have been one of the best artists Tucker employed.

Unfortunately, however, most Tucker china is not marked, and that leads naturally to problems of identification. Collectors can sometimes determine if a piece is genuine by matching it against the finely drawn sketches of Tucker ware in the old Tucker pattern books, which have been preserved at the Philadelphia Museum of Art. But since not every piece that Tucker produced is featured in the books, identification usually requires special knowledge of the characteristics of the ware. Tucker china was made in a large variety of sizes and shapes and for many uses. The great majority of pieces show a greenish tinge when held to the light. The glaze is usually transparent and clear, but where it has accumulated in denser masses it has a bluish tint.

The decoration of Tucker porcelain falls loosely into three periods. The first began in 1826, when the Tuckers moved their facilities from the shop to a building known as the Old Waterworks on Schuylkill Front Street in Philadelphia. The pieces created there are decorated with sepia or brown designs—sometimes floral sprigs or butterflies but more often landscapes with lakes, mountains, and small boxlike houses. Gold is used sparingly.

The second period started in 1828, when Tucker formed a partnership with Thomas Hulme, an affluent Philadelphian. William's artistic younger brother, Thomas, also joined the firm, and the character of the decoration improved. Sprays or groups of flowers became more common, and more gold was applied. Bird motifs were also used, but the Tuckers, true to their Quaker heritage, replaced the American eagle's thunderbolt with a pacific olive branch.

The Hulme collaboration lasted only a year, but in 1831 another prominent Philadelphian, Judge Joseph Hemphill, bought into the firm and built a larger plant at Chestnut and Schuylkill Sixth. The following year William Ellis Tucker died, and Judge Hemphill purchased his share of the works as well. He put Thomas Tucker in charge of the factory and directed him to produce china that Americans might mistake for the popular Sèvres ware imported from France. Many of these Tucker patterns have heavy gold bands, elaborate floral motifs, and, occasionally, portraits—all very much in the Sèvres style.

So successful was Hemphill at imitating Sèvres that collectors have had trouble ever since distinguishing between examples of the two styles. But there are ways to tell them apart. The sepia scenes common on earlier Tucker pieces sometimes appear on Hemphill's products, but never on Sèvres. The gilding differs—Sèvres is pure yellow, Tucker bluish purple. When similar pieces are held to the light, Sèvres has a yellowish hue, while Tucker looks characteristically greenish. Examination of the bases of vases with pedestals usually reveals other distinguishing characteristics. Tucker vases have a shallow depression on the bottom for the bolt that holds the base to the vessel; Sèvres vases have a similar but deeper depression. Sèvres bases are more heavily decorated than their Tucker counterparts; in addition, Tucker bases turn up slightly at the corners, giving the pieces a somewhat unsteady appearance not seen in the Sèvres vases.

Hemphill used his own fortune to keep the Tucker factory going through the bank failure of 1833 and the depression that followed. But a year after the judge retired in 1837, Thomas had to close the works. "I discontinued the manufacture of porcelain," he wrote, "and commenced ordering from Europe." The Tucker family had come full circle—from importing china to producing it to importing it again—but not without achieving William's goal of creating an American porcelain fine enough to rival foreign ware. Today, it's a fortunate collector who determines that he owns a true Tucker piece.

Betty Evanoff

All photos, courtesy Philadelphia Museum of Art. From top to bottom, left to right: Scent bottles with stoppers, 1837, given by Eliza Amanda Tucker; vase, 1835, given by Mrs. Alfred J. Brannen; fruit basket, 1832-1838, given by Anne Tucker Earp; vase, 1825-1838; sugar bowl and cup and saucer, c. 1830, given by John T. Morris; dinner plate, 1825-1838; identifying mark: Tucker & Hulme, 1828.

Sketch from the 1832 Tucker pattern book
Philadelphia Museum of Art

Through the frosted windowpane
A candle sends its welcome glow
While etching shadows on the sill;
A golden path falls on the snow.

Let this patch of warmth and beauty
Speak a message of good cheer
To each and every passerby,
"This is a special time of year."

So place a candle in each window
And let its radiant glow impart
A cheery welcome to one and all,
A Christmas greeting from the heart.

Becky Jennings

A Candle in the Window

Carols to a Neighbor

As long as a friendly light
Glows out your windowpane,
A soft petition into night,
Another carol we will sing to you,
A Christmas Eve refrain.

As long as one candle burns
From out your windowsill,
Through spatterfrost and ferns,
Another carol we will sing to you
Of peace and God's goodwill.

As long as we can see a star,
Radiant on your Christmas tree,
Spreading love and welcome far,
Another carol we will sing to you:
A promised child's Nativity.

As long as a single lamp
Shows eagerness through windowframe,
Of Magi march and shepherd tramp,
Another carol we will sing to you,
And hymn his blessed name.

Maurice W. Fogle

*Photo opposite
Fred Sieb*

The snowflakes ice the barnyard fences;
Inside, the embered hearth is warm;
The holly gathered from the woodlands
Is berry-red throughout the home.
The kitchen smells of ham, and sausage,
And bread that's baked with loving care;
The cedar bowed with satin ribbons
Holds popcorn balls and angel hair.

Christmas in the Country

The stars look down with quiet splendor
On candles gleaming through the pines;
The moon seems near in heaven's luster,
And how sublime its fullness shines!
Tonight the rural people mingle,
Unite their joys in glad refrain,
As carols ring beyond the chapel
With wondrous hope and peace again!

Inez Franck

A Stained Glass Window

High above the altar,
The sunlight beaming through,
There is a stained glass window
Of yellow, red and blue.

It is a thing of beauty,
And catches every eye
Of those who stop to worship
As they are passing by.

Made up of tiny fragments,
Which in themselves mean naught,
But when they're placed together
A thing of beauty's wrought.

So in our lives, the fragments
Of tiny deeds we do
Make up a life of beauty
With God's love shining through.

Katharine Gordon Gabell

Candlelight

Reluctant is the darkest night
To threaten bliss of candlelight;
For where the waxen tapers glow
Grim, questing shadows dare not go.

Soft candlelight betokens cheer
That beckons when the dusk appears,
And sends its gentle, golden beams
To set bright silverware agleam.

It bathes within its subtle fire
The household things of heart's desire.
Where scented candles bring delight,
Small children welcome stars of night

And love is ever present where
The charm of candlelight is there;
For living reaches heights sublime
When candles glow at twilight time.

Brian F. King

The Christmas Candle Legend

Agnes B. Nickl

During the Christmas holidays the many decorations which adorn the windows and doors of homes are truly things of beauty. Each decoration has a meaning all its own. The legend of the Christmas candle, seen in so many of our windows at this beautiful season of the year, tells an inspiring story.

Many years ago in a tidy little cottage on the edge of a village in Austria, a cobbler and his wife made their home. Their possessions were far from plentiful; but in spite of that, they shared what they had with others. Symbolic of their love and generosity for their fellowman was the lighted candle that they placed in the window of their humble cottage.

Over a number of years war, with its companions famine and destruction, fell upon the land. This little village suffered; yet, through it all, the cobbler and his wife suffered less than the others.

The villagers were puzzled about this and talked among themselves. "Surely, there is something special about them," they said. "They are always spared from our misfortune. Let us put a candle in our window and see if that is the mysterious charm."

It so happened that the first night a candle was lighted in the window of every home was Christmas Eve. Before the first rays of the morning sun showed over the horizon, a messenger rode into the village to bring the great news: peace had come to the land.

That Christmas Day there was amazement and awe in the hearts of the humble villagers. And, as they thanked God for the blessings of peace, they said to one another, "Let us always remember to light candles on the evening of Christ's birth."

Many years have passed since this beautiful custom of placing a lighted candle in the window on Christmas Eve occurred. The custom has spread all over the world, sending forth a message of love, hope and cheer.

SNOW ON A HILL

Come, walk with me to the tall, broad hill,
Which is now knee-deep in snow,
And see the white immaculate spread
That lies silently far below.

The bright sun casts a shimmering gleam
On the blanket so soft and white,
It decks the earth with a magic cloak
Which silently fell in the night.

The great trees stand tall and bare,
As if the land were deep in sleep,
Outlining beauty far and near
For the world of man to reap.

The snow-white blanket lay regally
Around each plant, white and serene,
The hills and rocks were hidden
As if tucked beneath a dainty screen.

Standing upon the hill in awe and wonder,
Drinking of the beauty given free,
A miracle sent down from heaven
To nature lovers such as we.

Mamie Ozburn Odum

Photo opposite
Fred Sieb

It is on the eve of Christmas,
In the now-forgotten days;
Country church lamps have been lighted,
And its yard is full of sleighs.

Horses tied there to the hitchracks
Now are wearing strands of bells,
Tinkling with their restless movements
To enhance the sound that swells
From the organ in the chapel,
And the carols of the choir.
They practice for tomorrow,
Seated near the blazing fire
Which is roaring now and snapping
In the tall, old Bridge Beach stove,
Stoked with wood chunks brought in autumn
From the nearby woodland grove.

And the picture in the darkness
That the lighted church now makes
Is the kind that leaves impressions
Which no memory forsakes.
It will come in recollection,
Through the years in many ways,
How the country church stood lighted
And its yard was full of sleighs.

Arthur Thatcher

Country Choir Practice

It's Christmastime, it's Christmastime,
The church bells say in every chime,
A time for work and care to cease;
Give praises to the Prince of Peace.

It's Christmastime, it's Christmastime,
A day for joy in every clime;
To celebrate the Christ Child's birth
And foster peace upon this earth.

Fir trees will shine with glowing light,
To cheer a stranger through the night,
And take a hand in brotherhood
For faith, for love and all that's good.

Carols will ring through cold, crisp air
While families gather everywhere;
And up above the stars will shine
Much brighter—'cause it's Christmastime!

It's Christmastime

Harriet Feltham

Photo opposite
H. Armstrong Roberts

An Artistic
Dream

Under a blanket of fairyland white,
The meadow is sleeping, no birds in sight.
Yet with their arms outstretched to God
The birch and the willow happily nod.

Nothing is stirring but the breeze,
Raiding the branches of the barren trees;
Winter weaves an artistic dream
When sunbeams glisten across the stream.

This is the magic time of the year,
This is when memories seem to appear,
Though blossoms vanish and chill fills the air
There is still beauty to see everywhere.

Caroline S. Kotowicz

I saw the winter magic,
One January day,
In every little snowflake
So frolicking and gay;
I felt the winter coldness,
The wind so sharp and shrill,
And watched the snow fall heavily
To cover glen and hill.

I thrilled to winter's sparkle,
The world so big and white,
The stars like gorgeous diamonds
Upon the winter's night;
The evergreens so lovely,
Amid the ice and snow,
And little dots of silver
To add a special glow.

I laughed at winter's boldness,
The freezing morning air,
And marveled at the snowdrifts
She built just everywhere;
A masterpiece that's certain,
A happy pleasant thought,
And nothing quite to equal
The magic winter brought.

Garnett Ann Schultz

Winter Magic

Ring On,
O Happy Bells

Ring on, O bells of gladness
With your message of good cheer;
Peal forth the merry tidings
In cadence sweet and clear.

Ring out the old year fading,
With its failures, let it go;
Ring in the joy and promise
Of a new year's rosy glow.

Chime forth your skyborne music,
With its intervals of mirth,
Arouse the aspirations
And hopes of all the earth.

Ring on, O bells of gladness,
With the joy you now impart;
Ring on and on, O happy bells,
And bring a song to every heart.

Joy Belle Burgess

For You at Christmas

May you have a Merry Christmas
With the love that Christmas brings;
May you celebrate the New Year
While the bells of gladness ring.
May your joyfulness be twinkling
As a diamond diadem;
May your days each be as shining
As the star o'er Bethlehem.

Irene Taylor

ACKNOWLEDGMENT

WINTER MAGIC by Garnett Ann Schultz. From SOMETHING BEAUTIFUL by Garnett
Ann Schultz. Copyright © 1966 by Garnett Ann Schultz. Published by Dorrance & Company.   Inside covers: Alpha Photo Associates

Gift Books Of Beauty And Inspiration

WINGS UPON THE HEAVENS features a series of 38 superbly illustrated Richard Sloan bird prints in rich vibrant color, each displaying remarkably detailed and realistic techniques in both bird and background representation. Accompanying these beautiful prints are a number of descriptive stories and accounts in poetry and prose relating inspiring visits to picturesque woodland, meadow and backyard bird communities. A gift book that will be enjoyed and shared by young and old alike. Hardcover—80 Pages—Only $3.95

UNTIL THE RACE IS WON . . . was their determined cry and VICTORY OVER ADVERSITY is now their legendary story. Share the interesting lives of famous American athletes who had to overcome physical, mental and other handicaps to succeed in the challenging world of sports. Relive the inspiring accounts of courage and determination of such greats as Gordy Howe, "Babe" Zaharias and many more—each a champion on and off the field. Illustrated with pictures of the history-making events and people. Hardcover—64 Pages—Only $3.75

FROM THE EDITOR'S SCRAPBOOK—For over 30 years people have inspired to the famous quotes and sayings of humanitarians, historians and humorists that have been regularly featured in our Editor's Scrapbook section of Ideals publications. And now, the "best" of these uplifting messages have been collected and warmly combined with a rich blend of vivid color photographs. The results—a treasured collector's edition that you and your friends will enjoy for at least another 30 years. Hardcover—64 Pages—Only $3.75

THE JOYS OF HOMETOWN LIVING takes a warm and intimate look at living in "hometown America." Color photos of homey scenes depict the simple joys of hometown life as meaningful poetry and prose discuss the rewarding feelings derived from the sense of neighborliness, security, friendship and relaxation that embodies small community living today. For those who live in small towns or big cities—but especially for those who love simple living. Hardcover—80 Pages—Only $3.95

A SEASON OF GOLD—A most inspiring and colorfully panoramic view of nature's most fruitful season—autumn, with nearly one-third of this beautiful gift book's pages featuring full color photographs and artwork. Blended among the pages of rich golden scenes of nature's splendor, "thoughts of gold" in both poetry and prose of such "masters of inspiration" as Frost, Dickinson, Keats and many others gently reflect upon subjects of the heart and soul. A year round source of meaningful messages to own or to give. Hardcover—80 Pages—Only $3.95

GOD'S PROMISES—This colorful gift book of beauty, in both word and picture, warmly presents an inspiring array of some of the most meaningful promises God has provided for us as an expression of His love and as a source of spiritual guidance for all who put their faith in Him. It stresses that most precious significance of His word as it applies to the everyday living of all Christians, offering a source of inner strength for troubled times, joy for happy times and restful assurance for all time. Hardcover—80 Pages—Only $3.75

For All Ages And Any Occasion

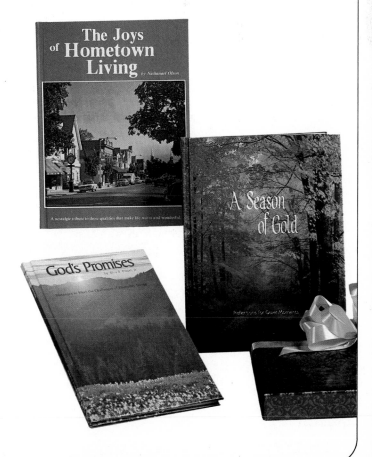

Christmas Begins And Never Ends With A Subscription To IDEALS

Here is the story of the real America, the good-news stories of down-to-earth Americans and the solid ideas and ideals they live by. Each issue of IDEALS includes a beautiful collection of full color photos—nature, people, homes, interiors, antiques—art reproductions that almost jump off the page, poetry, unusual stories and articles, and stories in pictures of the almost forgotten crafts of yesterday.

And every sparkling page of an IDEALS is absolutely free from distracting advertisements!

IDEALS is much more than a magazine . . . it's a delightful visit with the people who have made our country great—a renewed statement of faith in the customs, beliefs and purposes of yesterday. With each issue of IDEALS, keyed to the season, you discover anew the wonderful world of our fathers, of their regard for one another, of the honesty and love and steadfast belief in the good life.

There's color, pages and pages of glorious color scenes from all over America and around the world—the kind of photos you will want to frame and keep forever for sheer pleasure. But IDEALS is much more than a beautiful magazine. It's filled with stories and verse about the things and people and customs that have made our country great. It tells about the purposes and beliefs and daily lives of good people everywhere.

Future Issues To Be Enjoyed And Shared In The Months Ahead For Subscribers To Ideals

Jan.-Feb. 1978—FIRESIDE IDEALS—contains themes of home, friendship, country, winter's beauty. You'll enjoy a writing by Carl Sandburg on Abe Lincoln; a special feature on chess collections along with many more fine articles for year round reading enjoyment.

March-Apr. 1978—EASTER IDEALS embraces the religious significance of the season and the awakening of nature in the springtime. You'll enjoy the story background of Charles Wesley's hymn, "Christ The Lord Is Risen Today," and thrill to the beauty of springtime in the Rockies in "Wildflowers."

Every bimonthly issue of IDEALS brings more surprises and stories you'll want to save. That's why thousands of long time subscribers still have every issue they ever received. No one throws away IDEALS. It's too good a friend and companion to ever wear out its welcome.

And we are so sure you'll feel this way about IDEALS that we proudly extend to every new subscriber our personal

MONEY BACK GUARANTEE

If, after receiving the first copy on your subscription, you find IDEALS is not as beautiful and inspiring as you expected, just return your copy to us in its original wrapper marked "return to sender." We will cancel your subscription and the invoice due.

So strengthen your faith in country, home and the American way of life through the beautiful pages of IDEALS—enter your subscription today! You needn't send any money now unless you prefer. Simply mark the proper area on the order blank and we'll bill you later.

IDEALS SUBSCRIPTION PLANS

ONE YEAR.......6 issues as published $10.00
(A saving of $5.00 under the single copy rate.)

TWO YEAR........12 issues as published....................$17.00
(A saving of $13.00 under the single copy rate.)

THREE YEAR........18 issues as published.................$24.00
(A saving of $21.00 under the single copy rate.)

4 VOLUME........4 issues as published ....$ 7.50
(A saving of $2.50 under the single copy rate.)

PAY AS YOU READ PLAN
$2.00 per copy

Use the Pay-As-You-Read Plan: 1. Send no money now. 2. Expect the current issue, or any title you designate, by return mail, with an invoice and return envelope. 3. Remit $2.00 by return mail. 4. The next issue will be sent automatically; you needn't reorder each time. If you want to cancel your pay-as-you-read subscription, notify us at least three weeks before publication date.

IDEALS
1978 PUBLICATION SCHEDULE

Fireside Ideals	Jan.
Easter Ideals	Mar.
Neighborly Ideals	May
Countryside Ideals	July
Thanksgiving Ideals	Sept.
Christmas Ideals	Nov.

"Bound To Be Beautiful"
IDEALS BINDER

As rich looking as the six issues it holds with metal rods that eliminate punching. Stiff royal blue leather-cloth cover, embossed in gold. Yours for only $4.00. Hardcover 8½ x 11 inches.